Life Balance

A JOURNAL OF SELF-DISCOVERY

Life Balance

A JOURNAL OF SELF-DISCOVERY

CLARKSON POTTER/PUBLISHERS
New York

Introduction

Do you feel tired? Burnt and brittle from going too hard for too long? In work or relationships, managing family and responsibility, keeping the house clean and your social media presence palatable and pretty? Are you consistently resentful and irritable by the end of a busy week? Month? Year? So many of us are compelled to press through our daily lives at turbo-speed, packing as much as we can into twenty-four hours of precious time, day after day, without taking a breath for rest, relaxation, and re-calibration.

Balance is important. In order to lay the foundation for a healthy, balanced life, we must make deliberate efforts (over and over and *over* again) to focus on ourselves. This journal provides a safe space for you to find *your* way to life balance, using these three objectives as guideposts throughout your journey:

1 *Work-life balance:* In our digital age, it is harder than ever to unplug and turn your brain off when it's time to leave the office. Mindfulness of your actions when it comes to work-life balance is the key to breaking away from the chains that bind you to your work. You are more than your productivity. Set actionable goals to disconnect from work in the service of prioritizing your home, social, and inner life.

2 *Me time vs. we time:* Saying yes to friends and family is easy if you're an extrovert and crave connection, but don't forget the power of saying no to curl up with a good book or devote some time to a solo hobby. On the flip side, as an introvert, it might be hard to reach out for connection when you need it most. Challenge yourself to find the balance between alone time and the important relationships in your life. Lean on the ones you love and learn to lean on yourself, too.

3 *Emotional self-awareness:* In addition to managing your time, responsibilities, and energy (both mental and physical) more effectively, balancing your emotions will keep you more agile, less vulnerable, and able to face life's challenges with moxie and grace. When an intense emotion shows up and interferes with your ability to function, it may not be serving you. It is, however, trying to tell you something. It's important to be mindful of your own emotions in the service of figuring out what they mean, how you can effectively manage them, and make healthy decisions for yourself, even when you're feeling rage, anxiety, or shame.

Focus on these three areas of your life. Use the quotes, prompts, and blank pages in this journal for daily meditation, free-writing, creative pipe dreams, managing your hectic schedule, or simply as a reminder to carve out moments of mindful reflection during your week. The path toward a more balanced life begins with paying deliberate attention to work-life balance, self-care, and your emotions.

How to use this journal . . .

This journal serves a few purposes. First and foremost, it is a sacred space for you to express yourself as a means of finding your center. In her international bestseller, *The Artist's Way*, creative powerhouse Julia Cameron encourages those following her twelve-week program to journal each and every morning. The practice of writing "morning pages" asks creatives to free-write for no fewer than three pages in their journal; it is a valuable way of uncovering hidden stressors and fears that throw you off balance or, sometimes, values you didn't know you had! Committing to morning pages is a tool for anyone seeking clarity in life—not just for creatives on their artist's journey. This journal can be a place for you to write every morning or, if you can't commit to morning pages, try to write a few times a week.

Second, *Life Balance* is a reason to put aside some time for self-care. Throughout the journal you will find prompts and quotes that encourage you to think about mindfulness, self-care, and finding balance in your daily life.

Hint:
If you get stuck identifying how you feel, see the emotion index in the back of the book for a list of common feelings.

Finally, throughout the journal you will find exercises called "balancing acts." These pages will encourage you to analyze what's underneath your feelings of unevenness—whether it's an emotional imbalance, a social one, or a struggle with prioritizing, scheduling, and carving out time for yourself. These pages will encourage you to write about how you feel in order to find your way from the tip of a slippery iceberg back to stable, solid ground.

On emotions . . .

> "Nothing ever goes away until it has taught us what we need to know."
>
> —Pema Chodron

Many psychologists insist there is no such thing as a negative emotion. Emotions show up for a reason. They are little informants, guides that shed light on your hopes, desires, and values. We may not want to feel anger or fear or shame or disgust, but these emotions—however unpleasant—are indicators of what's important to us.

Our emotions are filled with information, but sometimes they balloon into something that feels too intense to manage, effectively throwing you off balance. Getting clarity on what your emotions are telling you is a valuable way to deflate the balloon just a little, giving you room to breathe.

Psychologist and author Dr. Tasha Eurich emphasizes the importance of asking "what" rather than "why" questions in exploring feelings. "Why do I feel so terrible?" may lead to negative, unproductive thoughts, while objective questions like "What are the situations that make me feel terrible?" help you stay focused on actionable, future-focused ways to combat unwanted feelings.

Another form of emotion regulation comes in what some psychologists call "opposite action." Has anyone ever suggested the simple act of smiling when you feel down as a way to pick yourself up? Next time you feel sad, try smiling for thirty seconds or more. You'll find it lifts your mood—even if it's only for a moment, even if it's only a *little* bit, this opposite action works.

Another example: When you feel intense anger and you want to scream or need a punching bag, channeling your calm, kind self to act in a manner that is opposite to your rage-informed urges will help take the wind out of your fury. Take deep breaths and hone in on things that make you calm. As difficult as it may be, it's an effective way to lower the intensity of your anger.

The "Balancing Act" exercises sprinkled throughout this journal will help you practice the skill of opposite action. When feeling an intense, unfavorable emotion, visit these pages to write objectively about what's going on for you, and take the time to focus on what might lift your spirits out of your slump, even if it's just a little bit—it's better than nothing at all!

With all of this in mind, go forth to find your balance. Practice deliberate self-care. Uncover what brings you clarity, calm, and back to center.

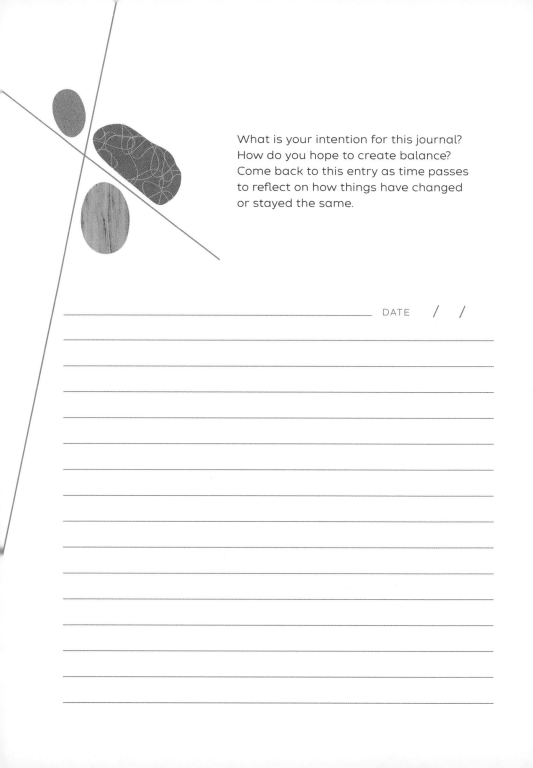

What is your intention for this journal?
How do you hope to create balance?
Come back to this entry as time passes
to reflect on how things have changed
or stayed the same.

DATE / /

*"Every single day, we can center
and prioritize ourselves."*

Lauren Ash

DATE / /

"Take care of yourself: When you don't sleep, eat crap, don't exercise, and are living off adrenaline for too long, your performance suffers. Your decisions suffer."

Ev Williams

What does balance look like for you? What has the greatest effect on your daily state of being? Food? Sleep? Frame of mind? Communication? Reflect here.

_____ DATE / /

Seek balance today.

"Take care of your creative health."

Nayyirah Waheed

_____ DATE / /

_____
_____
_____
_____
_____
_____
_____
_____
_____
_____
_____
_____
_____
_____
_____
_____
_____
_____
_____

In what ways do you feel off-kilter,
not centered? What are the physical,
mental, and social cues that hint at
a lack of balance?

DATE / /

*"If you're reading these words, perhaps it's because
something has kicked open the door for you,
and you're ready to embrace change.
It isn't enough to appreciate change from afar,
or only in the abstract, or as something that can
happen to other people but not to you.
We need to create change for ourselves,
in a workable way, as part of our everyday lives."*

Sharon Salzberg,
Real Happiness: The Power of Meditation

_____ DATE / /

_____
_____
_____
_____
_____
_____
_____
_____
_____
_____
_____
_____
_____
_____
_____
_____
_____

Balancing Act

Feeling off balance? What are you dealing with today?

Name a dominant emotion and reflect on what is weighing you down.
Be as objective as possible (you don't want to work yourself up!).

_____

_____

_____

_____

_____

How can the next thirty minutes feel more balanced? The next hour?
How can you plan for a better tomorrow?

_____

_____

_____

_____

_____

Write a list of five alternate feelings you'd like to tap into today (see the
emotion index in the back of the book if you need help):

1 _____

2 _____

3 _____

4 _____

5 _____

Balancing Act

How can you find balance today?

Name something with opposing influence here, whether it's an emotion, alternate priority, or distraction technique. Find something you can tap into to find more balance today, and label it:

_____

How can you carve out time for this opposing influence today?

_____

_____

How will honoring both sides of today's proverbial coin help you inch closer to a more stable, balanced being?

_____

_____

_____

_____

_____

List five opposite actions you can try today, in the service of finding balance:

1 _____

2 _____

3 _____

4 _____

5 _____

Close your eyes, place your feet
firmly on the ground, and take
a few deep breaths. How do you
feel in this moment?

DATE / /

*"Balance is not better time management,
but better boundary management. Balance means
making choices and enjoying those choices."*

Betsy Jacobson

_____ DATE   /   /

"Most of us spend too much time on what is urgent and not enough time on what is important."

———

Stephen R. Covey

How have you spent your time today?
If you could have done one thing differently today—
in the service of balance—what would it be?

_____ DATE / /

_____

_____

_____

_____

_____

_____

_____

_____

_____

_____

_____

_____

_____

_____

_____

_____

_____

_____

Seek balance today.

"*Balance is not something you find,
it's something you create.*"

Jana Kingsford

DATE / /

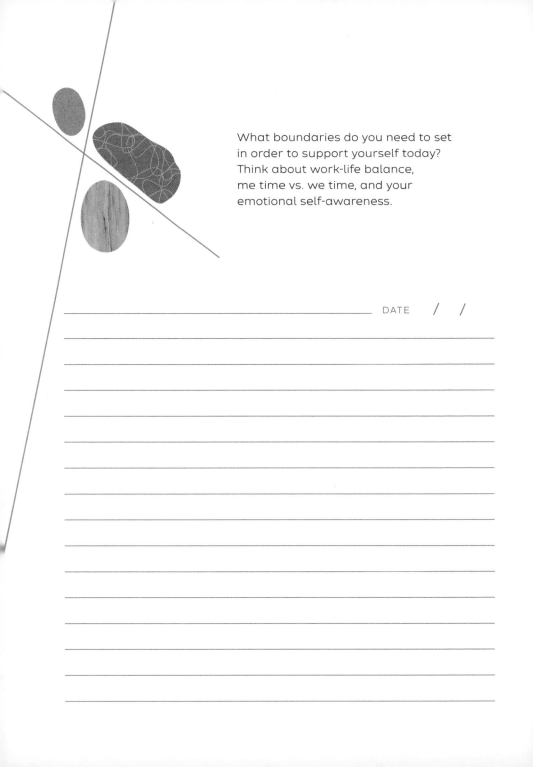

What boundaries do you need to set
in order to support yourself today?
Think about work-life balance,
me time vs. we time, and your
emotional self-awareness.

DATE   /   /

*"I think the key to doing a lot of different things
at the same time is not putting them in compartments.
Instead, see where the connections are made between them,
and how one can feed the other thing."*

———————

John Sharian

Reflect on the quote above. How might this apply to you?
Look for ways to connect the priorities in your daily life.

_____ DATE / /

Balancing Act

Feeling off balance? What are you dealing with today?

Name a dominant emotion and reflect on what is weighing you down. Be as objective as possible (you don't want to work yourself up!).

_____

_____

_____

_____

_____

How can the next thirty minutes feel more balanced? The next hour? How can you plan for a better tomorrow?

_____

_____

_____

_____

_____

Write a list of five alternate feelings you'd like to tap into today (see the emotion index in the back of the book if you need help):

1 _____

2 _____

3 _____

4 _____

5 _____

Balancing Act

How can you find balance today?

Name something with opposing influence here, whether it's an emotion, alternate priority, or distraction technique. Find something you can tap into to find more balance today, and label it:

_____

How can you carve out time for this opposing influence today?

_____

_____

How will honoring both sides of today's proverbial coin help you inch closer to a more stable, balanced being?

_____

_____

_____

_____

_____

List five opposite actions you can try today, in the service of finding balance:

1 _____

2 _____

3 _____

4 _____

5 _____

"At this moment, self-care to me means holding onto beauty and joy where I can find it and sharing those moments when I can. We need it to keep going."

———————

Celeste Ng

_____ DATE / /

_____

_____

_____

_____

_____

_____

_____

_____

_____

_____

_____

_____

_____

_____

_____

_____

_____

What does self-care look like to you? How can you hold on to moments of peace, joy, and confidence when you are feeling overwhelmed and off-kilter?

DATE / /

"Balance activity with serenity, wealth with simplicity, persistence with innovation, community with solitude, familiarity with adventure, constancy with change, leading with following."

Jonathan Lockwood Huie

Do you lean toward activity or serenity?
Constancy or change? Leading or following?
Reflect on the ways in which you can challenge
yourself in these arenas.

DATE / /

Seek balance today.

"We have overstretched our personal boundaries and forgotten that true happiness comes from living an authentic life fueled with a sense of purpose and balance."

Dr. Kathleen Hall

_____ DATE / /

When you feel yourself burning out, what excuses do you make to justify pushing through? How can you shift your priorities to ensure you're at your best?

DATE / /

"Burnout is about resentment. Preventing it is about knowing yourself well enough to know what it is you're giving up that makes you resentful."

———————

Marissa Mayer

Visit this page when you are feeling particularly burnt out. Is there anything you're missing out on or that you feel you're giving up? Reflect here.

_____ DATE   /   /

_____

_____

_____

_____

_____

_____

_____

_____

_____

_____

_____

_____

_____

_____

_____

Balancing Act

Feeling off balance? What are you dealing with today?

Name a dominant emotion and reflect on what is weighing you down.
Be as objective as possible (you don't want to work yourself up!).

_____

_____

_____

_____

_____

How can the next thirty minutes feel more balanced? The next hour?
How can you plan for a better tomorrow?

_____

_____

_____

_____

_____

Write a list of five alternate feelings you'd like to tap into today (see the
emotion index in the back of the book if you need help):

1 _____

2 _____

3 _____

4 _____

5 _____

Balancing Act

How can you find balance today?

Name something with opposing influence here, whether it's an emotion, alternate priority, or distraction technique. Find something you can tap into to find more balance today, and label it:

_____

How can you carve out time for this opposing influence today?

_____

_____

How will honoring both sides of today's proverbial coin help you inch closer to a more stable, balanced being?

_____

_____

_____

_____

List five opposite actions you can try today, in the service of finding balance:

1 _____

2 _____

3 _____

4 _____

5 _____

*"Self-care, at its core, is giving
yourself permission to do whatever
it is that you need to be okay."*

———————

Jen Gotch

DATE / /

_____

_____

_____

_____

_____

_____

_____

_____

_____

_____

_____

_____

_____

_____

_____

_____

_____

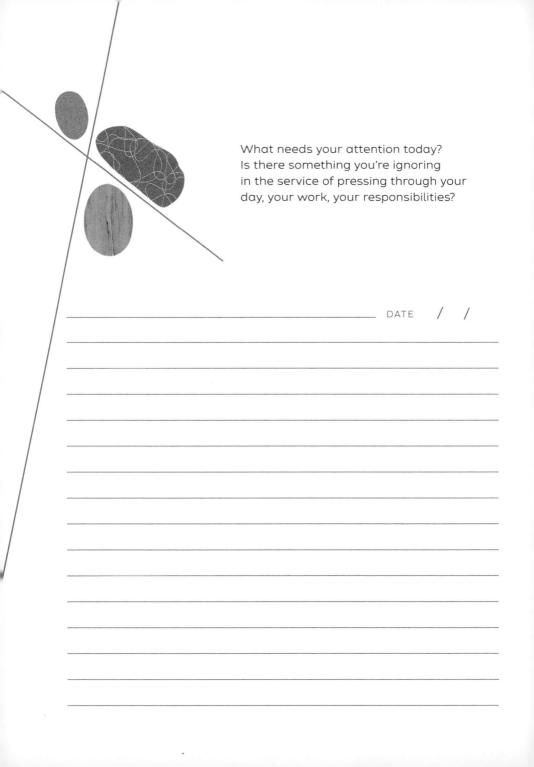

What needs your attention today?
Is there something you're ignoring
in the service of pressing through your
day, your work, your responsibilities?

DATE / /

"Between stimulus and response, there is a space.
In that space is our power to choose our response.
In our response lies our growth and our freedom."

————————

Viktor Frankl

Do you ever say yes to doing something or going somewhere when your brain is shouting, "No way!"? Reflect on what causes this disconnect. How can you slow down the time between stimulus and response to make more balanced choices?

DATE / /

Seek balance today.

*"Crying is a part of self-care.
It's one of the body's ways of releasing energy."*

Lalah Delia

DATE ___/___/___

What emotions come up when you are off-balance? How do you know when you need centering?

DATE / /

*"There's no 'should' or 'should not' when it comes
to having feelings. They're part of who we are, and their
origins are beyond our control. When we can believe that,
we may find it easier to make constructive choices about
what to do with those feelings."*

The World According to Mr. Rogers

Have you created "shoulds" and "should nots"
around your emotions? Explore any "shoulds"
and "should nots," where they've come from,
and what they might be trying to tell you.

DATE / /

Balancing Act

Feeling off balance? What are you dealing with today?

Name a dominant emotion and reflect on what is weighing you down.
Be as objective as possible (you don't want to work yourself up!).

_____

_____

_____

_____

_____

How can the next thirty minutes feel more balanced? The next hour?
How can you plan for a better tomorrow?

_____

_____

_____

_____

_____

Write a list of five alternate feelings you'd like to tap into today (see the
emotion index in the back of the book if you need help):

1 _____

2 _____

3 _____

4 _____

5 _____

Balancing Act

How can you find balance today?

Name something with opposing influence here, whether it's an emotion, alternate priority, or distraction technique. Find something you can tap into to find more balance today, and label it:

_____

How can you carve out time for this opposing influence today?

_____

_____

How will honoring both sides of today's proverbial coin help you inch closer to a more stable, balanced being?

_____

_____

_____

_____

_____

List five opposite actions you can try today, in the service of finding balance:

1 _____

2 _____

3 _____

4 _____

5 _____

"Suffering is our call to attention, our call to investigate the truth of our beliefs."

Tara Brach

DATE / /

_____

_____

_____

_____

_____

_____

_____

_____

_____

_____

_____

_____

_____

_____

_____

_____

_____

_____

Find some time to take a break from your to-do list today. Go for a ten-minute walk outside, take time to write a list of things you're grateful for, try holding plank for thirty seconds, or go for a jog around the block. Find mental and physical space to detach from your routine.

DATE /   /

"I've learned to accept—and even embrace—fear as a sign that I am being faced with an opportunity to grow and become a better person."

Shannon Mustipher

What do you fear today? How can you embrace it so it doesn't throw you off-balance?

_____ DATE / /

Seek balance today.

*"Having emotional intelligence
is equivalent to possessing a social
superpower. Learning to pay attention
and attune to what's happening for you
internally can help you communicate much
more effectively and authentically—in all
of your relationships."*

Shira Myrow

_____ DATE   /   /

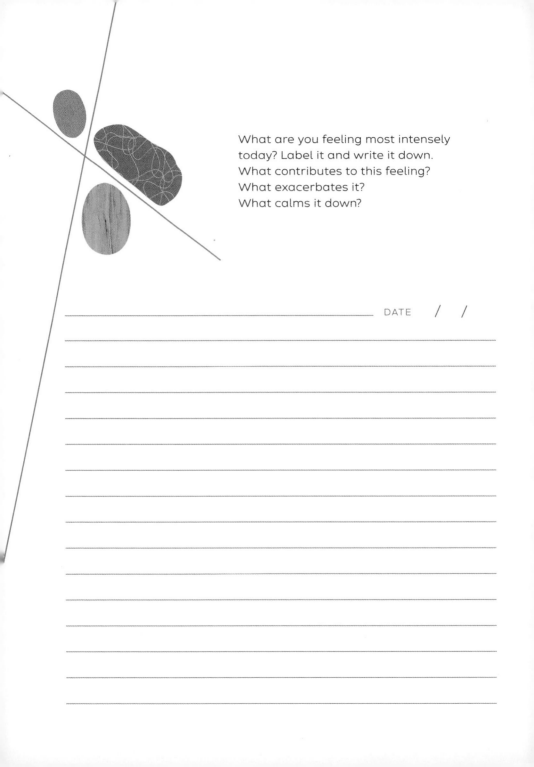

What are you feeling most intensely today? Label it and write it down. What contributes to this feeling? What exacerbates it? What calms it down?

DATE   /   /

"Pay attention to the subtleties of your body. Does your breath change? Explore. Does your heart race? Explore. How is your rest? Explore. More judgmental than curious? Explore. Ask yourself: am I feeling? Explore."

Dr. Crystal Jones

Mindfully explore your body today.
Write for five minutes (or more!) without stopping.

_____ DATE / /

_____

_____

_____

_____

_____

_____

_____

_____

_____

_____

_____

_____

_____

_____

_____

_____

Balancing Act

Feeling off balance? What are you dealing with today?

Name a dominant emotion and reflect on what is weighing you down.
Be as objective as possible (you don't want to work yourself up!).

_____

_____

_____

_____

_____

How can the next thirty minutes feel more balanced? The next hour?
How can you plan for a better tomorrow?

_____

_____

_____

_____

_____

Write a list of five alternate feelings you'd like to tap into today (see the
emotion index in the back of the book if you need help):

1 _____

2 _____

3 _____

4 _____

5 _____

Balancing Act

How can you find balance today?

Name something with opposing influence here, whether it's an emotion, alternate priority, or distraction technique. Find something you can tap into to find more balance today, and label it:

_____

How can you carve out time for this opposing influence today?

_____

_____

How will honoring both sides of today's proverbial coin help you inch closer to a more stable, balanced being?

_____

_____

_____

_____

_____

List five opposite actions you can try today, in the service of finding balance:

1 _____

2 _____

3 _____

4 _____

5 _____

"Feel it. The thing that you don't want to feel.
Feel it. And be free."

Nayyirah Waheed

DATE / /

What can you do for yourself today
in the service of balance?

DATE / /

"Whatever the present moment contains, accept it as if you had chosen it. Always work with it, not against it."

————————

Eckhart Tolle

What is going on in the present moment?
Is anything getting in the way of feeling balanced?
How can you work *with* this current moment
instead of *against* it?

_____ DATE / /

_____

_____

_____

_____

_____

_____

_____

_____

_____

_____

_____

_____

_____

_____

_____

Seek balance today.

"Stepping out of the busyness, stopping our endless pursuit of getting somewhere else, is perhaps the most beautiful offering we can make to our spirit."

Tara Brach, *True Refuge: Finding Peace and Freedom in Your Own Awakened Heart*

DATE / /

What are your priorities today?
Are any of them at odds with one
another? Close your eyes, place your
feet firmly on the ground and take
a few deep breaths. Re-evaluate your
priorities once you feel centered.

DATE / /

*"As you walk and eat and travel, be where you are.
Otherwise, you will miss most of your life."*

———————

Buddha

How can you press PAUSE today
to just *be where you are?*

—————————————————————————— DATE / /

Balancing Act

Feeling off balance? What are you dealing with today?

Name a dominant emotion and reflect on what is weighing you down.
Be as objective as possible (you don't want to work yourself up!).

_____

_____

_____

_____

_____

How can the next thirty minutes feel more balanced? The next hour?
How can you plan for a better tomorrow?

_____

_____

_____

_____

_____

Write a list of five alternate feelings you'd like to tap into today (see the
emotion index in the back of the book if you need help):

1 _____

2 _____

3 _____

4 _____

5 _____

Balancing Act

How can you find balance today?

Name something with opposing influence here, whether it's an emotion, alternate priority, or distraction technique. Find something you can tap into to find more balance today, and label it:

_____

How can you carve out time for this opposing influence today?

_____

_____

How will honoring both sides of today's proverbial coin help you inch closer to a more stable, balanced being?

_____

_____

_____

_____

_____

List five opposite actions you can try today, in the service of finding balance:

1 _____

2 _____

3 _____

4 _____

5 _____

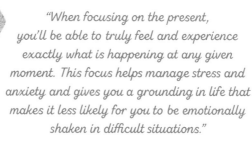

"When focusing on the present,
you'll be able to truly feel and experience
exactly what is happening at any given
moment. This focus helps manage stress and
anxiety and gives you a grounding in life that
makes it less likely for you to be emotionally
shaken in difficult situations."

———————

Joshua Sanchez

_____ DATE   /   /

How have you spent your time today?
If you could have done one thing
differently—in the service of balance—
what would it be?

DATE / /

"Give yourself permission to name what you need
without shame or guilt."

Alexandra Elle

How do you feel right now?
What do you need?

_____ DATE / /

_____
_____
_____
_____
_____
_____
_____
_____
_____
_____
_____
_____
_____
_____
_____
_____
_____

Seek balance today.

"When you're stressed out, scattered, or overwhelmed, finding your breath and centering your attention with mindful awareness can help you reset and re-anchor yourself. Even if you can't do a formal sit for twenty minutes every day, you can always take a five-minute break to breathe. Everyone has five minutes."

———————

Shira Myrow

DATE / /

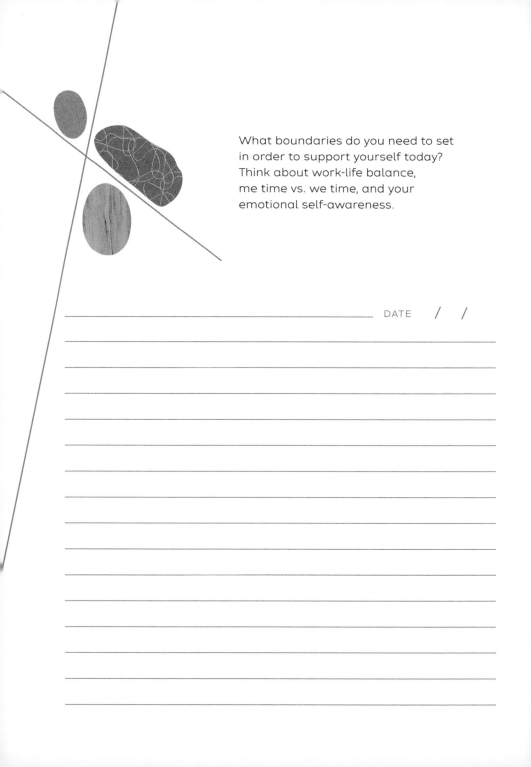

What boundaries do you need to set
in order to support yourself today?
Think about work-life balance,
me time vs. we time, and your
emotional self-awareness.

DATE   /   /

"The word 'happiness' would lose its meaning if it were not balanced by sadness."

Carl Jung

What opposing forces are necessary in order to find balance? How can you cultivate appreciation for "negative" emotions like sadness, knowing that they serve this purpose?

DATE   /   /

_____

_____

_____

_____

_____

_____

_____

_____

_____

_____

_____

_____

_____

_____

_____

_____

Balancing Act

Feeling off balance? What are you dealing with today?

Name a dominant emotion and reflect on what is weighing you down.
Be as objective as possible (you don't want to work yourself up!).

_____

_____

_____

_____

_____

How can the next thirty minutes feel more balanced? The next hour?
How can you plan for a better tomorrow?

_____

_____

_____

_____

_____

Write a list of five alternate feelings you'd like to tap into today (see the
emotion index in the back of the book if you need help):

1 _____

2 _____

3 _____

4 _____

5 _____

Balancing Act

How can you find balance today?

Name something with opposing influence here, whether it's an emotion, alternate priority, or distraction technique. Find something you can tap into to find more balance today, and label it:

_____

How can you carve out time for this opposing influence today?

_____

_____

How will honoring both sides of today's proverbial coin help you inch closer to a more stable, balanced being?

_____

_____

_____

_____

_____

List five opposite actions you can try today, in the service of finding balance:

1 _____

2 _____

3 _____

4 _____

5 _____

"Self-study is one of the most amazing things you can give yourself."

———————

Lauren Ash

DATE   /   /

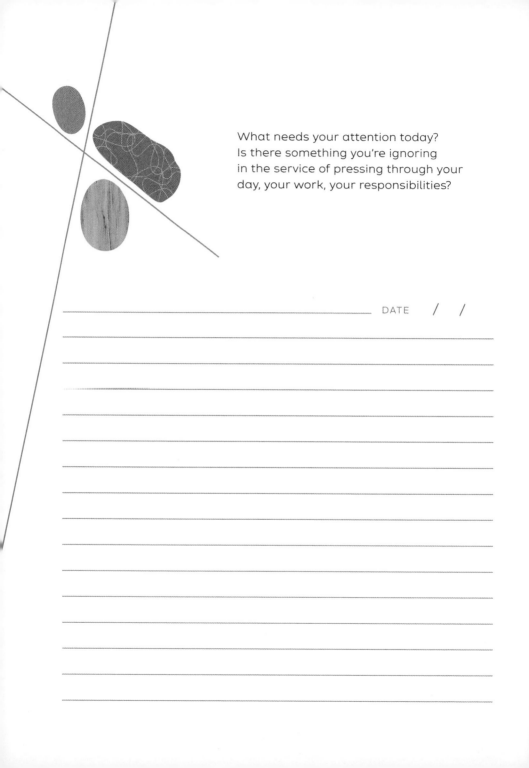

What needs your attention today?
Is there something you're ignoring
in the service of pressing through your
day, your work, your responsibilities?

DATE / /

"We can be sure that the greatest hope for maintaining equilibrium in the face of any situation rests within ourselves."

Francis J. Braceland

List some of your strengths in the space below.
Think about compliments you have received from
others in addition to the qualities you know you possess.
How do these strengths support you in times
of balance-seeking?

DATE / /

_____

_____

_____

_____

_____

_____

_____

_____

_____

_____

_____

_____

_____

_____

Seek balance today.

"We need to introduce a little balance into your life. Part of this balance means not missing out on some of the marvels of life around you, the fun, some excitement, or other challenges in life."

Catherine Pulsifer

DATE   /   /

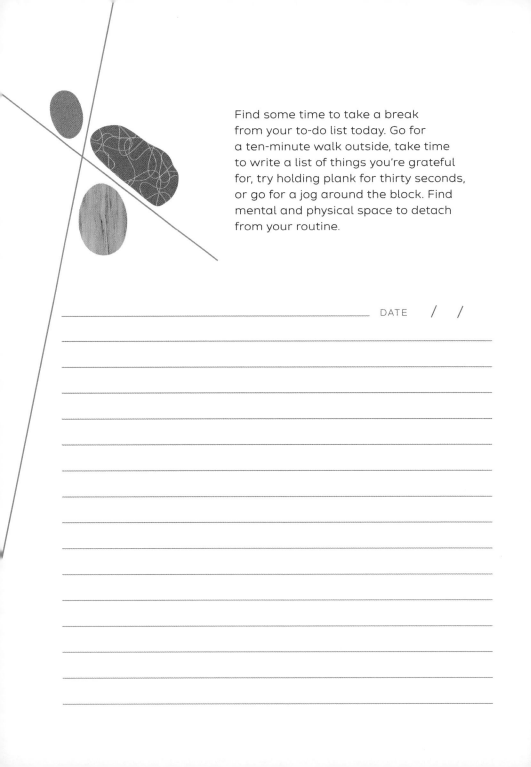

Find some time to take a break
from your to-do list today. Go for
a ten-minute walk outside, take time
to write a list of things you're grateful
for, try holding plank for thirty seconds,
or go for a jog around the block. Find
mental and physical space to detach
from your routine.

DATE / /

"Spend your free time the way you like, not the way you think you're supposed to."

———————

Susan Cain

Do you ever feel like you should be working/nurturing others/running errands/doing anything but relaxing during your free time? Why? Choose a day to combat that "should" with an action of self-care. Reflect on it here.

————————————————————————————————————— DATE / /

Balancing Act

Feeling off balance? What are you dealing with today?

Name a dominant emotion and reflect on what is weighing you down.
Be as objective as possible (you don't want to work yourself up!).

_____

_____

_____

_____

_____

How can the next thirty minutes feel more balanced? The next hour?
How can you plan for a better tomorrow?

_____

_____

_____

_____

_____

Write a list of five alternate feelings you'd like to tap into today (see the
emotion index in the back of the book if you need help):

1 _____

2 _____

3 _____

4 _____

5 _____

Balancing Act

How can you find balance today?

Name something with opposing influence here, whether it's an emotion, alternate priority, or distraction technique. Find something you can tap into to find more balance today, and label it:

_____

How can you carve out time for this opposing influence today?

_____

_____

How will honoring both sides of today's proverbial coin help you inch closer to a more stable, balanced being?

_____

_____

_____

_____

_____

List five opposite actions you can try today, in the service of finding balance:

1 _____

2 _____

3 _____

4 _____

5 _____

*"I think that the anxiety of time is often
what leads me to feeling unhealthy,
or to making poor decisions. But time is not
something we can avoid, so grappling with
it can be difficult. Learning to take time to do
what I know helps me, as well as taking time
to explore and discover in general, has helped
me have a healthier mind/body."*

Monica Mirabile

_____ DATE / /

_____
_____
_____
_____
_____
_____
_____
_____
_____
_____
_____
_____
_____
_____
_____
_____

What can you do for yourself today
in the service of balance?

DATE / /

"A further sign of health is that we don't become undone by fear and trembling, but we take it as a message that it's time to stop struggling and look directly at what's threatening us."

Pema Chodron, *The Places that Scare You*

What fears have been showing up for you lately?
What messages do you think your fear is trying
to convey? Reflect here.

_____ DATE / /

_____

_____

_____

_____

_____

_____

_____

_____

_____

_____

_____

_____

_____

_____

_____

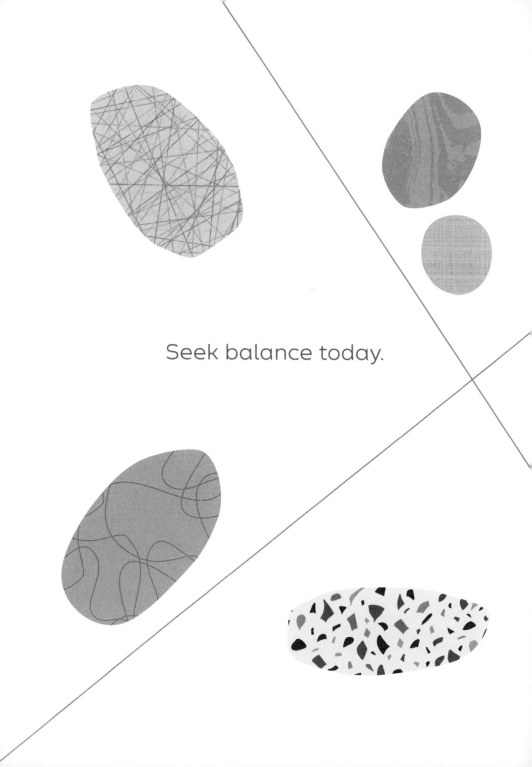

Seek balance today.

When you get overwhelmed, what are your go-to forms of coping? What are some additional coping mechanisms you can incorporate into your daily self-care routine?

DATE / /

"*You can't stop the waves,
but you can learn to surf.*"

———

Jon Kabat-Zinn

DATE / /

"It was all balance.
But then, she already knew that from surfing."

———————

Eve Babitz

Do you ever feel like the waves of responsibility, work,
social life, and emotions come crashing down on you all
at once? Learn to surf! Use the space below to list ways
you've learned to cope with feelings of stress and anxiety.
How do you "surf" through overwhelming moments?

_____ DATE / /

_____

_____

_____

_____

_____

_____

_____

_____

_____

_____

_____

_____

_____

_____

_____

Balancing Act

Feeling off balance? What are you dealing with today?

Name a dominant emotion and reflect on what is weighing you down.
Be as objective as possible (you don't want to work yourself up!).

_____

_____

_____

_____

_____

How can the next thirty minutes feel more balanced? The next hour?
How can you plan for a better tomorrow?

_____

_____

_____

_____

_____

Write a list of five alternate feelings you'd like to tap into today (see the
emotion index in the back of the book if you need help):

1 _____

2 _____

3 _____

4 _____

5 _____

Balancing Act

How can you find balance today?

Name something with opposing influence here, whether it's an emotion, alternate priority, or distraction technique. Find something you can tap into to find more balance today, and label it:

_____

How can you carve out time for this opposing influence today?

_____

_____

How will honoring both sides of today's proverbial coin help you inch closer to a more stable, balanced being?

_____

_____

_____

_____

List five opposite actions you can try today, in the service of finding balance:

1 _____

2 _____

3 _____

4 _____

5 _____

*"Our best work as creatives—
big-picture thinking, creativity, strategy,
ideas, connection—can only happen when
stepping away. Sure, I've had weeks that felt
nonstop, but I savor the days, weeks, months
when balance feels like the priority."*

Sarah Schulweis

_____ DATE   /   /

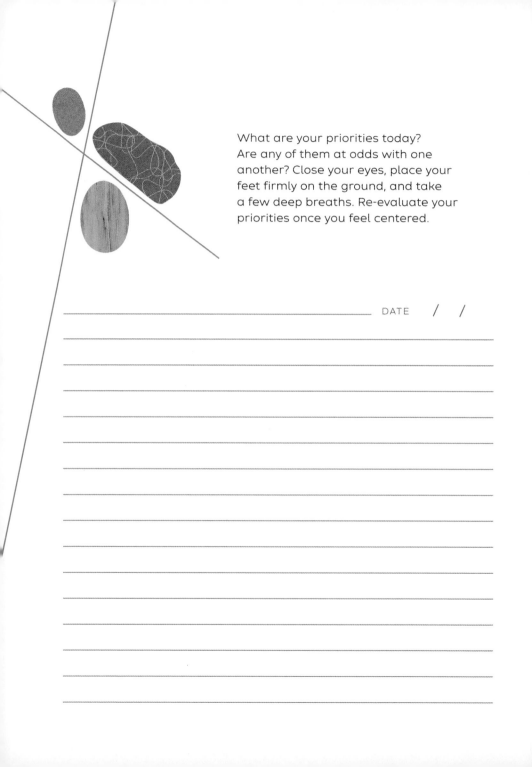

What are your priorities today?
Are any of them at odds with one
another? Close your eyes, place your
feet firmly on the ground, and take
a few deep breaths. Re-evaluate your
priorities once you feel centered.

DATE   /   /

*"Life is like riding a bicycle. To keep your balance,
you must keep moving."*

———————

Albert Einstein

Perpetual forward motion does not just apply to your
productivity. It applies to your emotional well-being,
your me time vs. we time, *and* your work-life balance.
How can you keep things moving in all of these
areas today?

_____ DATE / /

_____

_____

_____

_____

_____

_____

_____

_____

_____

_____

_____

_____

_____

_____

_____

_____

Seek balance today.

What will bring you back to center today? What do you need?

DATE   /   /

Balancing Act

Feeling off balance? What are you dealing with today?

Name a dominant emotion and reflect on what is weighing you down.
Be as objective as possible (you don't want to work yourself up!).

_____

_____

_____

_____

_____

How can the next thirty minutes feel more balanced? The next hour?
How can you plan for a better tomorrow?

_____

_____

_____

_____

_____

Write a list of five alternate feelings you'd like to tap into today (see the
emotion index in the back of the book if you need help):

1 _____

2 _____

3 _____

4 _____

5 _____

Balancing Act

How can you find balance today?

Name something with opposing influence here, whether it's an emotion, alternate priority, or distraction technique. Find something you can tap into to find more balance today, and label it:

_____

How can you carve out time for this opposing influence today?

_____

_____

How will honoring both sides of today's proverbial coin help you inch closer to a more stable, balanced being?

_____

_____

_____

_____

List five opposite actions you can try today, in the service of finding balance:

1 _____

2 _____

3 _____

4 _____

5 _____

"The best way to capture moments
is to pay attention. This is how we cultivate
mindfulness. Mindfulness means being awake.
It means knowing what you are doing."

Jon Kabat-Zinn

DATE / /

"Happiness is not a matter of intensity but of balance, order, rhythm, and harmony."

Thomas Merton

Reflect on the ways in which balance, order, rhythm, and harmony offer you happiness.

_____ DATE / /

_____

_____

_____

_____

_____

_____

_____

_____

_____

_____

_____

_____

_____

_____

Seek balance today.

"Life balance is a pursuit
and not a destination. In fact, a life
in balance often consists of many
seasons out of balance."

Troy Amdahl

DATE / /

Close your eyes, place your
feet firmly on the ground,
and take a few deep breaths.
How do you feel in this moment?

DATE   /   /

*"When work begins to get in the way of balance,
a radical notion of self-care, you may need a more
thorough visual of what your work is."*

———————

Marlee Grace, *How to Not Always Be Working*

Does the line between your work and play ever feel
blurry? Can you define what your work is? What it is not?

_____ DATE   /   /

_____
_____
_____
_____
_____
_____
_____
_____
_____
_____
_____
_____
_____
_____
_____
_____

*"Find your balance and stand with it.
Find your song and sing it out. Find your
cadence and let it appear like a dance.
Find the questions that only you know how
to ask and the answers that you are
content to not know."*

Mary Anne Radmacher

_____ DATE / /

"Vulnerability is the birthplace of innovation, creativity, and change."

Brené Brown

Your willingness to explore emotions, "shoulds," priorities, and the essence of what it means to seek balance is truly a vulnerable act. Think back to the reason you bought this journal. How has your willingness, openness, and vulnerability helped you seek change?

DATE / /

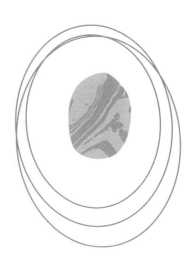

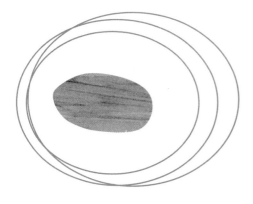

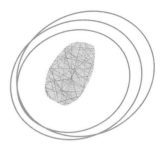

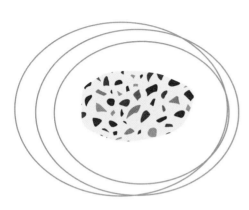

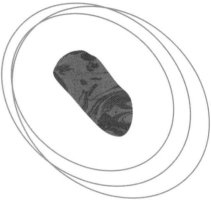

Emotion Index

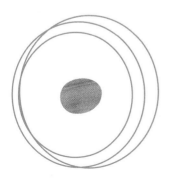

Here you will find a list of common
emotions. Feel free to add to this list,
as the nuances of what we feel are endless!

Adoration	Disgust
Affection	Dismay
Aggravation	Dissatisfaction
Agony	Dread
Alienation	Eagerness
Anger	Edginess
Annoyance	Embarrassment
Anxiety	Empathy
Attraction	Enthusiasm
Belonging	Envy
Bitterness	Exasperation
Calm	Excitement
Confident	Fear
Contentment	Fright
Comfortable	Frustration
Compassion	Fury
Defeat	Glee
Defensive	Gratitude
Delight	Greed
Depression	Grief
Despair	Guilt
Disappointment	Happiness

Hope	Rejection
Horror	Sadness
Hostility	Satisfaction
Humiliation	Shame
Hurt	Shock
Insecurity	Spite
Irritation	Stress
Jealousy	Surprise
Joy	Sympathy
Loneliness	Tenderness
Love	Tenseness
Neglect	Terror
Nervousness	Triumph
Optimism	Uneasiness
Outrage	Vengefulness
Overwhelmed	Vulnerability
Panic	Wariness
Peace	Worry
Pettiness	Wrath
Pride	
Rage	
Regret	

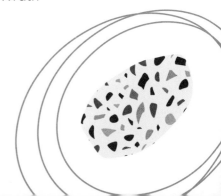

ISBN 978-1-9848-2390-8

Printed in China

Concept by ROBIE LLC
Book and cover design by Nicole Block

10 9 8 7 6 5 4 3 2 1

First Edition